Hearing the Stranger

Reflections, Poems, & Hymns

❖❖❖❖❖❖❖❖❖❖❖❖❖❖❖❖❖❖❖❖❖❖❖❖❖❖❖

MICHAEL HARE DUKE

SHEFFIELD
CAIRNS PUBLICATIONS
1994

© Copyright by Jim Cotter 1994

ISBN 1 870652 22 3

First published 1994

Further copies of this book are obtainable from
CAIRNS PUBLICATIONS
47 Firth Park Avenue, Sheffield S5 6HF

Printed by J. W. Northend Ltd
Clyde Road, Sheffield S8 OTZ

CONTENTS

Biographical Note v

Introduction vii

Women's Role. 1

Peace Poems 11

Power 19

Relationships 31

God's Paradox. 45

Songs to Sing 59

Connections 71

The Startlement of Shrines . . . 79

End Piece 91

ACKNOWLEDGEMENTS

WE are grateful to the following for their permission to include previously published material:

SPCK:
From *The Break of Glory* (1970)
Mine Own Familar Friend
One of the Nine
The Responsibility of God
Love

The Scotsman
Three Women for Peace
Ministers' Meeting
Peace Flowering
Patrick's Flame
Iona: Womb of a New Age?
Second Round?

The BBC
Good Day
Bridge of Night
Playtime
Alone

Harper Collins
From *Praying for Peace* (1991)
Desert Soil

Stainer & Bell
Wise One You Made Us to Share Your Delight
Sons and Daughters of Creation
Lord Whose Power Has Called To Being

BIOGRAPHICAL NOTE

MICHAEL HARE DUKE was born of Irish parents in Calcutta, India where his father built railways. Orphans of the Empire, Michael and his elder sister were sent home to England where they grew up in the care of a nanny. He was educated at Bradfield and Trinity College Oxford. Between the two institutions came a period as Midshipman and Sub-Lieutenant in the RNVR (1944–6). Returning from the War, he married his wife Baa in 1949. Four children and eight grandchildren later they are still in creative partnership. Trained for the priesthood at Westcott House Cambridge, he was a curate in St John's Wood, a vicar in Bury, Lancs and Daybrook, Nottingham. He was Pastoral Director of the Clinical Theology Association, 1962–64 then a consultant until in 1969 he became Bishop of St Andrews from which he retired on the 25th anniversary of his consecration, the Feast of St Ninian, 16th September 1994. Throughout his ministry he has been involved in various organisations concerned with mental health. He has also grappled with issues of peace and justice. In 1974 he became one of the founders of the Peace Project in the Scottish Episcopal Church; subsequently he represented the Episcopal Church on the ecumenical Committee for Justice, Peace and the Integrity of Creation in the Scottish churches and has been a member of the Peace and Justice Network of the Anglican Consultative Council. These interests have coloured the themes of this book that brings together a variety of writings from the last ten years.

Writer, broadcaster and author Michael Hare Duke has also been a member of the Liturgy Committee of the Scottish Episcopal Church and contributed to its Eucharistic rites, Ordinal and other new material. As he approached retirement, St Andrews University gave him an honorary Doctorate of Divinity.

INTRODUCTION

"Why," said the recording angel "do you think that you have a right to the scarce resources of the planet to multiply copies of your scribblings?"

It was a pretty aggressive attitude for an angel. It stung me into a militant response.

"Because I like them. I want to share some of the ideas with other people. I hope they will enjoy them and even find a helpful thought amongst them."

"You've had some of them printed in *The Scotsman*, you've sent the longer ones as Christmas cards to your friends. There are ones that have been around before and gone out of print. Is there no satisfying your ego?"

My mind ran over the various possible excuses. Socrates, when he defended himself to the Athenians, claimed that he had had an insistent inner voice, his daemon, who must be obeyed. It wasn't quite like that for me and much as I would have liked to claim direct inspiration, you cannot fool angles. He would think I was even more pretentious than he did already.

Since I had reverted to a classical precedent my mind went on to the great Greek dramatists, but no one could pretend that I was a latter day Aeschylus and in any case his plays had been directly commissioned to be performed at a religious festival. Only occasionally the BBC had actually asked for my lines. Mostly I had just wanted to put them down. Only later it had seemed to be a good idea to give them a wider circulation, in part at least at Jim Cotter's suggestion. How very much nicer he was than this angel, I began to reflect.

"Look at the price!" continued my tormentor. "Aren't we getting a bit above ourselves there, as well?"

"It's a very well produced book", I replied defensively. "Any author is lucky to have an editor, designer and publisher as good as the Cairns Publications team. I am very grateful to them for all the care they have taken and to the people who have helped in making the selection of poems to be printed. And before you get so thoroughly supercilious, I'd like to say thank you to the others whose work has contributed to the finished product. I have got a patient, efficient and perceptive secretary, Anne MacLehose, who has thought it worthwhile to put an immense amount of care into making sure that the pieces have come out looking as good as they can. Something like this doesn't happen as a one person show. It needs a lot of helpers including a wife who will feed you while you work and not try to rewrite the text.

The angel began to look abashed. There was a droop to his wing feathers. In a moment of insight a question occurred to me.

"The angelic choirs must need a huge repertoire; have you ever tried writing anything?" I had touched the neuralgic point.

"It never came out right" he said. "But it was not for want of trying."

I noticed a number of pinion feathers were missing and wondered whether they had been sacrificed to act as quill pens.

"Sorry I was a bit hard on you" he said. "It wasn't exactly the script I'd been given, but it's difficult to hold one's tongue and watch amateurs getting away with it when you have not had much success yourself!"

The picture of a vulnerable, envious angel was so surprising that all my aggression vanished. I was left with gratitude for all the people who had encouraged, shared in or excused the things that I had written in the past and those who for the future might find them helpful pointers on the way, or a stimulus that irritated them to do better for themselves.

At that point the dream was over and I woke up refreshed. I knew how the introduction should go and I sat down to the welcoming glow of my computer screen to type it.

MICHAEL HARE DUKE
Perth, May 1994

WOMEN'S ROLE

THE debate about women's role, particularly in the church, has rumbled on. I have been moved to anger, theological argument and laughter. There still seems to be room for the whole gamut of responses, to release us into the freedom which accepts the totality of human nature and refuses to run into a sexually divisive ghetto.

MALE AND FEMALE

God created human beings in his own image;
in the image of God he created them; male and female he created them.

Genesis 1.27

Here the poet myth-maker
discerns in the Creator's nature
the partnership of genders.
Others told the harsh dawn of human struggle,
where, the well of primal vision stopped,
each denied the other, unlike half;
wholeness severed by the fork-tongued lie.

Split within, humanity divided God.
The 'he' and 'she' of earthly disputation,
projected heavenwards,
found no echo in divine completeness.
The dichotomy bounced back
to rumble around sanctuaries
shrunk to the measure of a gender idol.

As, in an end-time, the Word took flesh,
the secret of the Eve in Adam
struggled to unite the refracted rays.
Old language bent and broke under the mystery,
the threadbare curtain split,
dry springs awoke.
Yet still the fear of sex, the politics of power
seduced a collusive church
to reaffirm the masculine.
hustling into heresy the hint of Motherhood.

Hedged with taboos
that hold an uncertain boundary
between sanctity and superstition,
the feminine stays veiled;
its invitation to the rich pasture of the Spirit
too great a threat to sharp analysis.

Like Jacob, man goes limping,
the eternal loser in the struggle
for mastery and dominion;
his choice to stay embattled
or else, disarmed, to embrace
his severed partner-self.

A LESSON FROM ZACHARIAH

Sacramentally assured, he stood,
Priest of the Most High, before the Lord.
His Mystery, crafted down the generations,
empowered the words and acts.
His self, subsumed into the Representative,
knew his essential core confirmed.

Through substituted hands,
the Godhead
King, Father, Lord of Hosts,
Victim and Priest
had ordained to fight and suffer,
mould, offer and command.

At the instant rite
God emptied himself into the bread and wine,
continually reproducing the great Exchange
of Bethlehem.

'This is my body':
The ordered phrase leaped out like fire
to touch his substance.
Penetrated by the unsuspected possibility,
his curtained sanctuary was torn
into awareness.

Bride and mother,
his own hands prepared food for the family;
he heard his gentle voice
tell of forgiveness, promise birth
into a new creation.

Graceful, embracing gestures
validated the flowing vestments:
the feminine he had denied
danced in his being
and the laughter of the Spirit broke
the imprisoning waters.
Borne on the flood of insight
he could glimpse the deeper unity of two made one.

Whole within, he scrawled across the empty page
the ecstatic truth
'His name is…
She',
and a new language sang
from his loosened tongue.

LETTER FROM PERGAMUM

The Vicarage
Pergamum
25th August 49

Dear Chloe

You have no idea what life has been here since that dreadful letter arrived from Jerusalem saying that Paul had won his motion in Synod on a unanimous vote. How could James have been so blind to the heritage of the past as to have allowed the flood gates to open and let Gentiles in without condition? I suppose these liberals are influenced by the current fashion for the multi-cultural unity of the Empire. Look at the way all sorts of people become citizens these days with no reference to their ancestry. But why does the Church have to follow the way of the world? Should we not be different?

Unless we take care all the ideas of a pluralist society will crowd in and wash away what is most precious in the tradition of our fathers. We have forgotten the holy gift of the Covenant and turned to an ideology that believes that God has no favourites. This is not the way that in the past Israel stood fast against the pressure from the country folk to worship Baal. Where would we be now if that dyke had broken? It is by holding on to the purity of our heritage that we remain faithful to God.

For the church to lose its fundamentally Jewish character would mean absorption into the mishmash of religions which wash around the Empire. You can see the effect from the fact that there is a move among some of the new converts to sue the Pergamum Church Council for insisting, before the goal posts were changed, on circumcision. They are saying that it is not just the doctors' fees but the pain and indignity for which they wish compensation. If basic theological truths can be changed with the wave of a voting paper, they argue that they were misled by the church authorities who maintained the absolute requirements for baptism. We understand that lawyers are already working on the case.

As well as the strain of this, which of course is putting my poor Antipas under terrible stress as the Vicar, they are holding obscene parties where pork is served to celebrate the new "liberation of theology".

Our Church Council have met and agreed that it is unthinkable that we could ever accept the ministry of a pig-eater. How could we allow the Mysteries to be desecrated by hands which had carved pork. I can't even bear the thought of exchanging the Peace with a brother or sister who might have been guzzling bacon the night before. That kind of behaviour is only the tip of the iceberg. There are appalling stories circulating already but I will not shock you by repeating them.

I understand that all over Asia Minor the traditionalists are looking to establish a network of the "Full Circumcision Party". Would it be possible to found an FCP branch in your area? It would give you access to a kosher bishop whenever you needed and, more importantly, you would be able to decide for yourself whether he was kosher or not. This is one way of keeping safe the universal and indivisible truth until these innovations have passed. We must not be tainted by streaky liberals. Hold fast and remember Ezra who cleansed our shame when he made the renegades divorce their Gentile brides at the time of the return.

Your devoted
Euphemia.

INCARNATION

"Ugh, disgusting, spit it out!"
"Don't touch it, dear!"
"Now go and wash your hands!"

A clinically unsullied childhood teaches that dirt is 'bad'.
Bodies regrettably excrete
but we can keep the guilty secret.
"Set your minds on things above",
where nothing nasty happens.
A split world
hides the unacceptable behind a pall of reticence.
The good child obeys the monkey-law,
eyes, mouth and ears sealed in unsullied piety.

"Do you suppose my holiness,"
enquires the Creator,
"is blind or deaf?
Does my tongue stumble over
 the names that you deny?"

"Blasphemy!" cries the priest,
"This is no God – a tempter seeks to penetrate
the barriers.
The tender flock will be destroyed,
they'll wander into chaos,
unholy lust will breed a hellish harvest.
If once the dam-wall breaks,
licensed feelings, bucking all control,
will flood the sanctuary."

The Christ of God
is gloriously and sordidly enfleshed.
The Word which sang creation into being,
enacts the interplay of dark and light.
Emerging from the womb
placenta-fed, bloody and joyous,
he declares his reign
over the breadth of human happenings.

Through turbulent, disturbing years of ministry
he touched the putrid flesh of lepers,
welcomed the rejects as friends
and died an outsider's death.

Women who had shared his company
breaching society's taboos,
were left to bury him and bear
an ambiguous witness to the empty tomb.

Religion thought its work was done
as spirit split from flesh;
till the great sigh of dying breath
ripped through the screen which hid
the empty show of holiness.
Temple and tomb alike
discarded, God claims his whole creation.

Partners in the dance
of resurrection,
opposites are paired;
sharp colours of contradiction
reform in a kaleidoscope
of new perceptions.
Light draws brilliance from its sister, shadow.
Body and spirit build a complementary beauty.
Resting a moment from the demanding clay
the Potter laughs to see his hands
drip glory.
The unspeakable is blended into poetry.

WISE WOMEN

The camels halted, transfigured by starlight.
Questing nostrils found no special scent to identify divinity.
The envoys, dismounting, rubbed the sand from their eyes,
the ache from their limbs.
Delving in saddlebags they found
the mysterious gifts.

"Here's the gold of power, mobilised for peace.
The children of the world should not grow up
to fight and suffer violence.
A woman knows the wickedness of war
therefore I offer up its underpinning wealth".
Matching the gift, her golden hair
flamed like an angel's anger.
"They shall not pass to restock armouries.
My city will obey the just command
to serve.
New songs will oust the martial airs.
In our time, love must overcome."

"The golden gift is dangerous alone
it needs a complementary mode,
anointing the world with justice."
Slender brown hands held out the myrrh.
"You will not sheathe the sword by lordly fiat
nor win peace like an empire.
The confidence of needs fulfilled,
riches shared – not snatched by competition –
    nurture true hope.
I bring a mother's longing
to see all children fed."

"Sisters, the gold and myrrh both cast a shadow.
Justice in chains
invites trumpets to sound a violent end to tyranny.
I bring a fragrant dream,
the incense of a whole creation
blended in harmony;
unsullied earth,
air without poison
taste of sweet water.
Together they sustain the House of Life
beneath whose roof the scales of justice
balance as gifts meet need,
and peace can flower in freedom".

"My heart could wish it" sighed the mother,
"but how can such things be?
Your symbols show a kingdom
unlike the powers that dominate this world".

"We sense the rush of blood,
the stab of pain,
darkness at noon,
a desolate cry, before it is accomplished.
The knowledge of the wise defined our gifts;
their meaning hovers at the edge of understanding,
hinting at a perplexing glory."

Reaching his infant hand to touch the hard-edged toys
the child was hurt
and celebration darkened into tears
until a woman's comfort
embraced the pain of God.

PEACE POEMS

THE day's news of violence or visits to places in distress, like Northern Ireland, have produced ideas that I have wanted to share. Some have been published, others have been sent to friends, so that we could inform each other's compassion. The forms of violence take so many turns that in this field there is always something new to be said.

DESERT SOIL

In the Gulf War

I've shut the door,
bombast and debate stilled to silence.
Sand clouds from the challenging tanks subside
into the Wilderness of Presence.
No bush bursts into flame,
but, instant as a heart beat, sounds the human cry
"Sir, come down,
come down before my child dies".

Once it was a father, pleading for a son in Capernaum.
Now the intercession serves the mother
whose boy smiled at the camera,
on mannequin parade with his platoon,
displaying the gear
-designed to thwart the gas and germs
of a mad scientist's war.
It's spoken in Iraqi, Kurdish, Arabic
and all the Babel tongues that sound
across the lands of Abraham's Sons.

"…before my child dies".
The hunger-gaunt faces
and match-stick arms
make another plea
from the parched earth of Africa,
as climate, debt or political corruption
dry the dust of death.

The desert's holocaust
is summoned by human choice.
Oil-rich consumers and their armaments
have robbed the poor.
Only the small change of charity
funds the famine appeals
because the wealth of nations
is spilt in the sand
of economic empire.

"Come down...".
No clouds will part to save us.
The divine response of healing
is not a thunderclap of might
but the soft rain of human tears.

Then we must make the choice
which either lets them run into the ground
or feed a watered garden.
Only beware, the time is short
before God's children die
and take our future with them.

THREE WOMEN FOR PEACE

The risks of Bosnia

A campaign general,
the First plans where to concentrate her fire
for maximum effect.
the mission accomplished will square the cost of casualties.
Crises demand leadership.
Though pax britannica has gone
the style lingers.
When control has slipped and war is wild,
force must contain mad dogs.
Strike hard for peace!

The Second spends herself in tears,
for her sisters' devastation,
fearful that she and her children
may be broken on the same wheel
of senseless revenge.
She nurtured her family
in a world green with hope;
it has grown tinder dry.
Better to die before the universal flames
engulf her home?

For the Third the question burns,
"Is the labour of history bringing to birth
a bloody misshapen end,
or does the outcome wait
its mothering?"
At the dark edge of exhaustion
can sufficient love draw the bitterness
and sing peace in the battle?
Squinting down the sights
can hard eyes blink and recognise
the target merge into the friend denied?

She hears the transforming music.
Accepting its commitment
she opens her arms, raises her head
and summons her sisters to dance
to Sarajevo's cello.

SHADRACH AND FRIENDS

*King Nebuchanezzar made an image of gold and demanded that all
people worship it when they heard the full royal orchestra play.
Shadrach, Meschach and Abednego were victims of the Decree, but came
safe through the trial.*
                                                    Daniel 3

Sadistic tyranny devised
a holocaust to music.
Piety comforted, "Don't worry,
God will save his chosen".

Anaesthetised with faith,
in ethnic allegiance
the Babylon Three stood rigid
defying the orchestra's cue.

"Kill".
The age-long fury of impotent authority
stoked the flames to white heat
that froze the victims' blood

It fried their executioners,
yet perhaps swooping wings
would snatch them as they fell,
God's SAS highlighting the miracle
by split-second timing.

At the touch of fire,
faith and flesh melted.
Then their spirits leapt to see the stranger.

Not spared, but accompanied,
they found in the furnace,
the Temple of Resurrection
and walked free
from the taint of devastation.

PEACE FLOWERING

The Arab-Israeli accord

You never know with God.
Covenants carry double meanings,
his and ours.
Is it a Promised Land or a prison?

Unreliable as British Rail
he offered an excursion out of Egypt,
that took forty footsore years to arrive.

"Birth" and "Death" redefined
darken the poetry of his purpose.

Yet at the pit of ambiguity,
clear as a rainbow arching a rain-drenched sky,
gunfire has melted to smiles
between old enemies.
The tears we thought wasted,
are poured from the safekeeping of his goatskin bottle
to water the desert into life
with roses of Shalom.
Promises take time.

PATRICK'S FLAME

In the shadow of the old gods
the faith of Ireland
kindled the Gospel fire
across the map of Europe.
By coracle to Iona, down the Rhine,
beyond the Alps, through Bobbio to Salzburg
the Spirit's flame spread by the beacon zeal
of Columba, Columbanus, Gall and Fergal.
The civilising Word gave the wild energy of the warring tribes
a centre,
tamed anarchic powers and harnessed them to
reasoned statesmanship.

After a thousand years
the shadow's power reclaims the land of faith.
The holy ruins of the ancient priories stand
shamed by the debris of the bomb attack.
There's confusion:
the gods of blood usurp the trappings of the Trinity;
the name of Jesus is part of the graffiti.
Violence spewing from extreme pulpits
is translated into gunplay on the streets.
Terrorists who die
demand the rites of Christian burial.
The bandit's balaclava does duty for a martyr's halo.
Candles that burned for loyalty and justice
are choked by sulphur from the brigand brands
of greedy extortion and naked power.

Nobody listens:
the easy accusation of 'traitor' gags dialogue.
Law and order is denounced as cloaking collusion
with a wider violence.
Mistrust devalues state security,
so black markets provide protection
at mafia prices.

The policeman's child
watches his father check the family car
for booby traps.
Flak jackets and guns in duty hours,
for the rest quick wits and sharp response
to parry the threat that does not sleep.

A violent killing is the excuse for death.
A mother mourns her son,
then sees his brothers
trapped in the game of violence
played by the paramilitaries.

By Patrick's courage
an Easter flame once leapt on the hills of Meath
to break the pagan night
and build a unity.
The flavour of history has soured.
A catalogue of wrongs, spiced with religious slogans,
divides the embittered tribes.
Fear stifles,
anger and strident accusation deafen
negotiation;
in the shedding of blood is no redemption.

Repentance is the key,
sorrow for power abused, lands stolen,
rights denied.
This is the alchemy to shift the nightmare to a golden dream.
In the exchange of God's forgiveness
there still might be a wild procession dancing
up a green hill:
politicians behind a fiddler singing together
"We were wrong!";
the violent texts of sermons folded into paper darts;
infants with balloons joy-riding in the armoured cars;
men dispensing bullets melted into toys;
masked men, turned wise,
and bringing gifts – mortars, semtex and kalashnikovs –
to lay them at the altar;

women laughing in celebration of joy reborn
and at the head, the Child
whose eternal wisdom knows the exit from death's valley.

Dreams have a power.
Might Patrick's flame rekindle
and from the crucible of pain
distil wise folly for a fear-split world?
Ireland of the Saints,
reclaim the human gifts of God's salvation.
Beyond all tears
find laughter to lift the portcullis
of unhealed memories that
exclude the stranger
and emprison neighbours in anger.
Victims in the land for which we weep,
take your power and lead us into life.

Belfast, 1991

POWER

POWER frightens us so we do not discuss it. But we are seduced by it and play games of hide and seek. The crucified king offers a totally new vision where strength and weakness, success and failure change place.

THE CHILD

Vulnerable, dependent
the infant waits
to be touched by kindness, suckled by love.
He wields no power
except the persuasion of fragility.

Yet the tyrant trembled
when the unwise magi revealed
the star's secret.
Blood brothers of all Terror
the troops moved in to liquidate
the destabilising Child.

Subversive in survival,
he staged a comeback from Egypt via Nazareth
and fell victim to the violence
of the Imperial Peace.
Yet Christmas celebrates the Coming
as the prelude to love's victory
which splashed the sky with glory.

I have seen fragility
flattened by juggernauting power,
shanty towns bull-dozed,
tongue-troubled teenagers
put down by adult arrogance.
Pain and frustration are cashed in tears and anger,
but always beyond the edge
of disappointment, hope glints.
No one need choose to stay a victim.
The vulnerable can blaze a trail to undefeated living,
when they have learned the mystery of the Child.

Once in a way the pattern breaks through history's distortions
and shows a generosity not abused.
The Christmas game's recast from older styles,
no longer shepherds blindfolded by dark
hunt the treasure hidden in a trough,

but freedom's flowers spike the cannon,
songs sweep the gun-fire into silence,
and Wenceslas' horse snorts defiance at the stabled tanks.

Quickly the world withdraws
into the reflexes of domination.
The politics of vulnerability pose too high a risk.
Yet when the multinational chain
fetters the tycoon's spirit
and the iron of the market
enters his soul, the simplicity of the Stable
seems luxury. It's just the place
for millionaires to leave their gold,
kings their crowns and
torturers their tools.
"God rest you merry" brays the ass
mistaking penitents for gentlemen.

SHALOM

"Peace" sang the angels.
Heaven which knew what they meant
approved.

"You must be joking" said Joseph
bleary-eyed from the strain of the birth,
woken by jostling cattle
and intrusive shepherds.

"Good thinking" said the Colonial Administrator,
planning a new frontier road,
"Free movement for the legions
guarantees peace".

Herod had a temple to build.
Innocent deaths might be the regrettable cost
of security for the grand design.

Down the generations,
Justice has hanged
those who broke the peace,
as though their necks would mend it.
Across the bodies of rioters and mutineers
muskets have sung the triumph of Law and Order
to citizens of goodwill.

Contemporary Christmas wishes
on regimental cards
decorate the General's cabinets
Operation Apocalypse, filed Top Secret, locked within.
Through the vigilant night jet engines
hum their battle hymn,
hijacking the angelic choir
as overture to Star Wars.

The vulnerable Child
offered another Peace
green with the promise of Spring:
our human fear has sought salvation
in the threat of Winter.

Yet still the stable Birth stirs a dream –
of power without oppression
generating liberty;
the whip of wealth no longer cracked for exploitation
but broken into common good;
the old embittered histories
retold with laughter and compassion.

The moat which separates the dream from action
is muddy with the flood of double meanings.
Yet in the Word is the release of language;
his angels invite us to cry 'Peace'
with tongues untied from stammering ambiguity
and with them harmonise the cosmic 'Yes'
which all Creation waits
to set it dancing.

STAR SURE?

More myth than history,
declaring only the direction of their coming
the strangers have travelled the by-ways of Christmas imagery
We've crowned them kings and found them names,
Melchior, Caspar, Balthazar,
conveniently one to each gift
embellished with sermon-sized significance.

The story-clouds rolled back, we find an earthier tale.
Astrologers, star-stirred but then misled, by false assumptions,
to a foreign court,
unwittingly bring death to an innocent generation.
But what they give to the surprising King
are all the symbols of their magery and stock-in-trade of power:
the mastery of gold, the astringent myrrh
and incense whispering of worlds unknown.

The story bites wherever domination
becomes the game:
when power manipulates the facts,
harnesses misery to gain its ends
and twists the lives of others.
Voters conned by specious manifestos,
workers denied just wages,
humanity wasted in prison or queues of unemployed,
the dying children of the desert;
all are victims of a system which could save
but chooses to serve its own advantage, claiming to know best.
Justified by superior technology
it arms itself to live by others' death.
Exploiting wealth to purchase its desires
inviting worship of its way of life
which disinfects the air-space from destruction,
it plays the sorcerer's part
to give the illusion of control.

The strangers gave the tackle of their magic to the Child,
to make them harmless toys.
But were they only half-wise men,
apt to read the skies but blind
to the wiles of statecraft,
so they became unaware informers,
ambiguous worshippers guiding the Terror by their naïveté?
What must we keep and what surrender
to learn from their example?

Lord of a world in darkness,
before we confuse the sky with satellites,
thinking to make the stars redundant,
guide us by the sacrifice of love.
Give us the daring of those who journey
along the path of open danger,
where once the fantasy of Pharaoh's might was drowned
and slaves found freedom.
Help us risk our treasure-store of power,
the convention of security based in others' fear.
When we can see no star
give us the courage to lose our way, rather than lose our souls
corrupted by immobilising information
that claims the illusion of omniscience.

We have no certain vision:
tomorrow comes new-born,
loosed from arthritic dogma,
let's dance to meet the dawn.

BRIEF SIGHTING

The Philippines 1992

For a fortnight in late November the members of the Peace and
Justice Network of the Anglican Communion met in the
Philippines for their seventh consultation. On each occasion they
reflect together on the situation in the provinces that they
represent, but chiefly they try to experience the reality of the

place where they are meeting. This coloured my Christmas thoughts for 1992.

> Heirs of the Magi, we've pursued the light
> of Peace and Justice
> not for one star-led journey
> but in recurrent meetings round the globe.
> This year the Philippines:
> our jet-lag outslept,
> following precedent, we explored the capital,
> as once Herod's Jerusalem, so now Metro Manila.

> Jammed traffic pulsated pollution,
> in stores and restaurants Christmas carols
> provided musak to spend to.
> Candles flamed in the great Basilica,
> where, shuffling on their knees, the devout
> adored the Sacrament;
> in the patio, pathetic crones begged for pesos,
> the National Lottery promised salvation by lucky ticket,
> whores sold their bodies and their health;
> in air-conditioned offices transnational deals
> arranged the rape of resources.
> Desperate poverty danced with corrupting wealth.

> On the margin, fisher folk
> had built a bamboo web
> of alleyways and dwellings
> hung precariously over the river.
> A community of resistance,
> they claimed ancestral rights to water
> pillaged by industrial powers.
> Their children, like otters,
> dived through the floating garbage.
> Others, without benefit of water
> breathed the stench and picked the rotting surface
> of Smokey Mountain.
> We had found the kingdom of survival,
> not of hope reborn.

Under the obedience of the quest,
we set out for the hill country.
A determined Filipino,
successor to the earlier camel drivers,
sat at the wheel of a hard-mouthed bus.
Ridden by hearty farmers, bringing home a pig,
compressed by mothers with their attendant brood,
the seats, weary of human weight,
repelled, jarring the spine, contorting shoulders.

Through the day we travelled
pausing to water a thirsty engine,
and after each crash of rocks,
to count the wheels.
Darkness engulfed us
while the road snaked upward
for four more precipitous hours
of earthquake-damaged track.
Safely arrived, the exhausted driver
crushed the water pipe that fed our hostelry.
And so, unwashed, to bed.

Clear mountain air and the clamorous bell
of an insistant Anglican woke us
to a day among terraced rice fields
and people hungry for the Gospel birth.

Herod's troops were still on active service,
informers, CAFGU, monitored our course.
The community beyond both tyranny and violent resistance
built reconciliation with the same patient care
their ancestors had cultivated the mountain face.
In their church the crucifix had snapped when, in a 'quake,
the east wall collapsed.
Bullet holes in the roof recorded last winter's confrontation
between a Government brigade and the New People's Army.
yet they had declared Sagada a Zone of Peace.

We found no star or stable, no pious ox or ass,
though there were engaging pigs, bred for roasting.
Trivialised in Manila's Xmas tinsel,

here, the solemnity of Christ's coming
set the stark earth aglow.
Mary's strong daughters cradled human dignity,
ready to defend land or freedom.
Weaving a pattern of justice,
their mothers' love confronted exploitation's lust
and touched the hills with glory.

'PEACE TO MEN, WHO ARE GOD'S FRIENDS'

Terror, blood and guns, spatter the headlines.
Peace has failed again.
Wherever there's a border
Patrols go out expecting enemies.
Even sedate suburban doors need chains against intruders
Surviving is a full-time occupation in a warring world.

Fight the vandals! Beat the bomb!
Righteous reinforcements, come!
Stamp out violence, blast away
Sweep the field and win the day.

Sweating after victory,
How different is the conqueror from his foe?
Can he stay uncorrupted?
Will his children learn the oppressor's goose-step
till someone else spins Freedom's wheel
and brings them tumbling down
black over white?

Peace is not the bloodied sword snapped back into its scabbard,
the bad-man buried with a gut-full of goodies' lead.
That's just the prelude to another war.
Peace is the Child, armoured in vulnerable flesh
greeting as 'Friend' the scowler, the pain-bringer
the man in the wrong uniform.
There is no right of entry.
No just demand enforceable at law
Only a gift to change
The universe from foe to friend.

Peace is made with open hands
Nothing dominates or binds
Link us Lord in love's exchange
Where brothers meet and power is strange.

SYNOD SONG

Militancy corrupts the business of assemblies.
Marshalled for action, the parties parade for weapon inspection;
riflemen draw magazines of quick-fire argument,
sappers prepare to explode cherished belief with their
    heartless science;
cavalry sabres are sharpened to slash confidence.
Devotion to the self-selected cause, mistaken for
    divine obedience,
fosters the brash crusader's confidence
that crushed skulls honour the Crucified
and manipulated ballot boxes glorify eternal Truth.

When pious clichés are deployed to claim God
as the totem of the embattled tribe,
the way is open to the corrupting zeal
that tortures for truth,
fights heresy with fire
and hangs in the name of Justice.
Arrogant minds reading God's purpose
from their answer book,
mishear the import of Love's question
which asks not "What?" but "How?"

So come, Liberator Spirit,
unbind the prejudice, disarm our fear of strangers,
entice us into the holy celebration of unlikeness.

TEMPTATION

There are plenty of things a Messiah might do,
a magical fix, a political coup,
or a pinnacle jump in full public view.

But when they are over, what's left to be said?
"We outgunned the rebel and now he is dead."
"We're sorry, the stones are just very stale bread!"
And "Don't you try jumping, you'll fall on your head!"

The suggestions were offered, but Jesus declined,
avoiding the trap of the secular mind
that persistently looks for a ploy it can find
to beat its opponents and show them as blind.

When love is the player, the game is not 'won',
no losers must forfeit their place in the sun;
but, building together, God's work is begun
and the 'what' matters less than the 'how' it is done.

Not a place at the top, but God's worship and praise;
the word of God's wisdom, not food that decays;
grace steadily given, not tricks to amaze;
so, Messiah has mapped out the heavenly ways.

RELATIONSHIPS

How we treat each other is the heart of human living. It is also the test of christian discipleship. Damage inherited from our individual or corporate past holds us back from the freedom of engagement. What questions need to be asked to open the way to a more rich exchange between friends or strangers?

ALONE

How lonely is silence?
If I feel shut in, cut off from company,
then it's a prison cell
and I use noisy crowbars to crack the stillness,
turn up the radio, phone a friend,
or choose a tape to fill the void before I sleep,

But it can be another way;
the stillness of solitude can be the place of meeting;
go deep within and I can find
myself – rich in memories
equipped with fire and feeling,
free to scale the heights of imagination,
free to grow.

It's a fine invitation,
but do I fear I'd meet another self,
unreconciled, the child of shadow,
who might emerge in silence?
Is noise needed to obliterate his cries
and business to bolt the dungeon door?

The self I fear, will dominate my life;
my energy expended most on his containment,
and I will miss the creativity of silence.

Lord Christ, you went alone into the wilderness
to find your truth.
Help me to dare the solitary night;
to journey inwards,
to transcend the fear, because you travel with me,
And so, in loneliness, befriended,
in the night, enlightened,
may my fears and hopes,
my fullness and my poverty,
be formed into the light and shade of glory.

THE SAFETY OF CHILDREN

A cancer of the soul devours the land
where violence, greed and lust
prey upon children.
The naked boy strangled in English parkland,
twinning a maimed child in Sarajevo,
accuses the universal murderers.
In Brazilian streets, nicknamed 'gabiru', the sewer rats,
a new generation are hunted down
because they claim the right to crusts
that wealth and crime have cornered.

The privacy of British homes
conceals the perversion of groping adult hands
that leave violated daughters to scream in silence;
shame, confused with loyalty, twisting their identity
away from wholesome love.

Distorted by the fear of strangers,
children grow up in drab containment
drilled to yell and run
from an encounter with unlikeness.

We have smudged innocence,
violated helplessness, corrupted trust.
We wait our children's absolution to free our action,
the song of their forgiveness to exorcise
our death-obsessed imagination,
their unspoiled delight
to dance us under hope's rainbow
into the fragile birth of a new dawn.

THE SPACE BETWEEN

"Don't come too close!
I love you, yes of course I do;
but I can only give when you allow me space.
When you take over, and my will becomes
a reflex of your strong desires,
then you engulf me.
Your dominating insecurity
sucks out the marrow of autonomy from my core being.
For love's sake, so that I can breathe,
don't come so close!"

"You're far away;
I need to know you're there, where hand can reach;
where you can hear a cry.
I feel you go into the frozen north lands;
you say it's just a summer holiday.
Space may give room to breathe, but distance kills."

There is no rule which measures in objective metres
the space that joins or separates.
The gauge is feeling and the gulf's as wide or narrow
as inner trust can stride
or fear falls short.

Love is a liberation
which by grace permits inclusion.
Yet once I say "It's mine" and keyed up with anxiety
lock fast the door,
its essence dies.
Yet there's another twist in the dark path:
for if I say "Go free, free as the air"
back comes the answer, "I knew you didn't care!"

A children's game of hide and seek,
but barbed with adult malice,
blocks out forgiveness.
The loving-space becomes the battleground.
It is no longer safe to show one's weakness

in case it's turned to accusation:
"That's right, lay on the suffering;
you won't catch me in a web of guilt".

So distance seems the only remedy – get out of earshot
There you can't offend and jibes cannot reach.
The space becomes a moat; there's nothing left to do
but write 'Trespassers excluded' on smooth castle walls.

So many dead-ends in the maze of love
might justify despair,
and yet a dream stays with us – 'We shall be known' –
not through a prying inquisition that usurps control
but with delight that sees all and rejoices.
So the indwelling and our own remove
into the house of the beloved pose no threat.
There is a way to be embraced and liberated.

The love of God dissolves the space between
without annihilation
We are not suffocated at almighty breasts,
but find an equal friend in a cool garden,
or beside us on a painful road
after a day that has eclipsed our hope.

Then we must ask, "Is he a learner too,
discovering from fresh pain the surrender of omnipotence
to those who have not learned to use their power,
yet must be free to grow?"

As we play in such relatedness
exploring how our God might show himself
a lover and a saviour
can human hurts get healed?
Is this the way the deadly interchange becomes
the loving-ground of mutual indwelling?
The battle-cries still sound – "Too close!', Too far away!"
but woven into song
celebrate a new hope of risen life
that makes it safe to offer all who come
our vulnerable, cross-grained selves in open undefended territ'ry.

PEOPLE

So many people!
Crowding the supermarket, pushing along the pavement;
babies, born every second, swell the statistics
of an over-populated planet.

People invade, their voices penetrate the ether,
floating through space, faces materialise on my screen, –
and yet it's lonely.
Until out of the crowd comes
someone who wants to know me and be known.
That exchange is where I become human.
In today's business
whom have I let over the threshold,
into the living space of feeling?

People have passed me in cars, served me in shops,
    phoned me for information,
but where has the spark leapt
to connect brother and sister?

Lord, in the lonely crowd,
one woman touched you,
and in the flash of recognition she was healed.
Through a haze of heat and faces,
you stopped your journey to focus on one man,
tucked in a tree.
You called his name and his whole world was changed.

Light up my eyes with love,
and recognition, so that each day is rich with meeting.
Touched with others' life,
I'll be drawn from isolation into human company.

LOVE

I looked for love in a mother's face.
She kissed her baby and held him tight.
The world was warm with a summer sun.
But the heart has a winter, a weariness of doing,
when the sense of demand freezes the gift
and care is measured out in grudging ounces.
The lips still call him "Darling"
but the eyes say "Clamouring brat".

I looked for love from a father's strength;
A hand to hold up, a voice to steady.
But the words became harsh and accusing:
fear and jealousy barred the way
that trust might have travelled.
An enemy carried his son to bed
and tenderly kissed him goodnight.

I looked for love in a woman's arms
She found what I wanted and gave it me lightly.
"We will be happy in pleasing each other.
Today is enough"
But tomorrow came and I was cheated.
I learned the lesson that love is disengagement;
A clinging, then a pain.

Love is the shock of eyes turned away
Love is the heartbreak of parting
Love is the hurt you feel by the open grave
Love was my god – and the world is empty:
My God why have you forsaken me?

Beloved Son, nailed and derided.
The harvest comes after the seed has died.
The slippered comfort of self-tolerance is suffocation.
I run away from truth into death by pretence.
Teach me to love even when the pain is fierce
Or in the nothing of the darkest night.
Take love into the shadows where self-hatred lurks
and trust that you were worth the death of God.

Yet love does not take away the pain,
It gives a purpose to the holding on
till you can say "It's finished, victory's won;
Scarred hands receive my spirit".
So sorrow becomes luminous joy.
The mourner claims his blessing and is comforted
with Glory which opens midnight windows on Eternity.

Love waits to show himself without disguise
Our anguish stands between and blinds our eyes.

THE INTRODUCTION

Andrew had a gift for introductions.
He spotted the boy with the loaves and fishes;
he guessed that Peter would want to meet
the Rabbi from Galilee.
Perhaps there were failures too,
friends who said "Thank you,
we'd rather stay at home";
embarrassed young
retreating into anonymity.
You are never sure what people want to do.
There's risk in pushing privacy too hard,
but reticence leaves the door tight shut.

Once I was a sailor, not a fisherman, in Edinburgh.
Evangelists, soul-spotting, took me back for tea.
Asking if it was "Well wi' my soul",
one pressed a calendar of coloured texts into my hand,
"Here laddie, hang this on your fo'csle".
The Colgate smile parroted the naval word
but never cared to learn a ship's geography.
Concern or manipulation?
I'd never volunteer for God's scalp-hunters
but I admire their guts.

History records the ambivalence of mission
in many modes.
Cultural imperialism made a shotgun marriage
of commerce and Christianity.
Now we fumble to untie the knot.
Brass Buddhas are no longer made in Birmingham;
Christ casts the Canterbury-woven clothes.

The Christian soldiers hesitate to march.
Crusading's out; but going round
the table of 'dialogue' seems only half-committed.
Like wind-tossed branches, the bishops' crooks
shake in disagreement
as positive assertion fights with honest doubt
to be the accepted style.
What meaning's left for mission?

Andrew returns; "Why don't you bring
your questions to the Master?"
I am led not to the Examiner who must be satisfied
    with answers
but to a friend who washes my dilemmas.
Where I have been mistaken, chosen wrong or
    failed to understand
forgiveness frees for action.

"Come and see" –
what I discover sends me running
to fetch friends and family
and let them meet the Lord.
He knows who will deny, who love, who lead;
beyond our faults he gives the hidden name,
that quarries 'Peter' from the sand of Simon.
Ours are the introductions; his the work.

MINE OWN FAMILIAR FRIEND

On one of his teaching journeys round the villages he summoned the Twelve and sent them out in pairs on a mission.   Mark 6, 7

Why did it have to be him, Master?
There are twelve of us in the company,
and you had to send us out together,
walking the roads, sharing the hospitality,
telling your message side by side.

John would have been a considerate companion,
we could have shared our fears and known a comfort
from the growing bond between us.

Peter would have led us into difficulty;
there might have been storms and troubles,
but we'd have laughed.
His spirit would have stayed us both against the opposition.

Judas would have made practical decisions.
He'd have been the leader,
but I could work with someone I admire.
But this man…

I have to apologise for him;
Let them know that we are not all like that.
When he preaches, it's a jumble of ideas
toppling out of a jar.

Along the road he's silent when I want to discuss,
chatty when my heart's too full for words.
He snores at night…

I'm not criticising, master.
Of course you know what's best.
Or perhaps it was just that you thought I didn't matter.
You'd fixed the others up and someone had to go with him.

But was it all a waste?
Will people be put off,
because they saw his foolishness – and my impatience too?
For awkward ways stopped me from doing all the things I could.

Some days I felt like praying for a stiff bout of dysentery
to lay him low
and set me free to be myself a while.

Of course you are right.
We need each other's help.
Something you said about humility,
I don't quite remember.
But, please, next time, it would be nice
if you could find someone to bring out the best in me.
I hate to see the mission fail or look foolish
just because we don't agree…

ONE OF THE NINE

As they went they were cleansed…Then said Jesus "Were not ten cleansed? Where are the nine?"　　　　Luke 17, 14 and 19

Call me ungrateful then!
Of course I know I'm healed –
the stinking blight that burrowed in my flesh
has gone.
I'm not a leper now – don't keep reminding me.
The priest said "Clean"; there's nothing more to add.
But I had dreamed that in the single word
all would be given back.
I'd prayed that the Shepherd
would help me find green pastures.
For a moment the promised land seemed
lying at me feet.
The Healer touched me –
my flesh had felt no wholesome hand
for three years past;
from him flowed the sense of power.
Even before I looked,
I knew his springs of life had
welled into my stagnant being.

After that moment, I believed the world had changed.
But now I'm back, here in the village,
my corn-filled Canaan

looks as bleak a stretch of Dead Man's Gulch
as any leper walked.
The sunny welcome soon gave way to all the
quarrels in the family –

Not just the brothers' rivalry we'd known,
but now resentment that the walking corpse
had come to claim his place among the living.
Had not young Joash there let his mind wander
over my pretty wife,
waiting to do his lusty duty by a brother's widow?
Even my father's eyes close on the dream
of quieter days when my quick temper
did not disturb the evening by the fire.

When all my mind was filled with one desire
to find that I was clean,
I had forgotton there was more to mend
than just the flesh.
One miracle is not enough
to put the world to rights.
I've learned the cruel lesson
that it's all diseased.
Life's way is lethal.
In the race you mend a broken leg
Only in order that your skull may split
against a jutting rock.
Call me ungrateful then!
It's hard to thank the power that saves
you for another dose of death.

What's that you say?
Yes, there were ten of us and one went back again
to see the Nazarene.
Don't ask me what he found,
Glib phrases like 'a faith'
are Greek to me.
He must have felt this disillusion too,
discovered that ideals are not for living.
You know him then?

Gone? that's sad to hear –
and by a slow disease.
That's just the thing I meant –
always the dark that swallows up the light
Why then does each one strive for life
against the certain cure of endless sleep?
Don't tell me he found peace
you either go on fighting for the impossible
or settle for the second rate
wrapping bare shreds of dignity around your wasted hopes.

O heart of mine that grapples with despair
you shape your wants to air-borne castles,
fantasies to fit your whim.
No wonder that they take no hold in hard reality.
But there is hope
when we can find our joy
not in imagination, but in facts.
When all my view was focused on the loss,
the hurt, the emptiness of me
I felt a prisoner, trapped in my weakness
by a hostile world.
Somewhere a light has dawned
which throws the shadows now a different way.
What seemed like bars have the power to bend
as saplings which allow a path.
I need not hate the obstacles
which once spelt out defeat.
Words will not compass the new certainty
which makes me give of love;
but this I know
that I can breathe and move
under a load which if I felt alone
would stifle me in waves of self-despair.
A hand has touched me
and a faith has flowered
to give me healing that can hold to life,
beyond the circumstance that each day brings
breaking a way into eternal light.

GOD'S PARADOX

THE Birth and Death of Jesus continue to perplex us. We want charming beginnings and happy endings but God is identified with humanity at its most needy, physically and emotionally deprived.

This is why the Gospel is Good News for those who acknowledge their poverty.

THE PRESENT

"God, who creates out of nothing, who almightily takes from nothing and says 'Be!', lovingly adds 'Be something even over against me'. Wonderful love, even his omnipotence is under the power of love."
Sören Kierkegaard

Children respond to boundaries; someone in charge
makes them feel safe.
"Time for bed" brings the day to a reassuring close.

So we grow to look for the hand on the tiller,
the firm grasp on the wheel.

Does an expanding universe require
a Mind in omnicompetent control,
mastering the logarithms of infinity,
alert to the sparrow's fall?

Would that imply a universal plan
devising good and evil,
computing coronaries or allocating births?

"Enough of arid arguments; gut faith demands
the power of God to hold, sustain his world."

Then Christmas dawns and draws the curtain back
to show a helpless child.
Dependent on a woman's breast,
the baby Jesus liberates our power;
We can't off-load the weight of choice.
There's terror in the gracious gift
for those who fear the forces
surging in themselves – and others.
Already we have glimpsed destruction
poking its warhead from the stocking.
Yet hands that will one day bear the scar of nails
present us with the competence to be
the arbiters of this world's life or death.

The Christmas crisis comes love-wrapped
and labelled 'Happy Future',
signed with the omnipotent autograph,
Immanuel.

WHERE IS THE CHILD?

Natural guesswork guided the caravan
to Herod's palace gate.
the prophet's scroll pin-pointed Bethlehem
The travellers glimpsed him,
the head of the secret police
never knew that his blood-bath was futile.
The Child had slipped away.

Tyranny feels the threat of a birth
which lifts the catch of guilt and fear and hate.
What's left to check the beast that lurks in man?
Gods should be kept sky-bound;
let them loose to dignify humanity and nothing's sacred!

But where's the Child?
He fled from Bethlehem; in Egypt a short-stay refugee;
no fixed abode in Palestine;
at last we managed to get a golden crown over his head
and set him in a jewelled Institution.

A recent report suggests a change of scene.
they say he may be found among the people
I most despise.
The golden glory has broken from the frame we'd set it in.
Sightings are possible
Among Marxists and managers,
bishops, bureaucrats, bombers, bums –
beneath each label, where real being hides,
there is the Child.

But you and I will not discern
the hope or joy
until he's born within.
His eyes in ours must recognise
himself – the God in Man

The Child is everywhere.
Lord Jesus, Come!

THE LIGHT SHINES IN THE DARKNESS

*"The light shineth in the darkness and the darkness comprehended it
not." or... "did not master..., grasp..., understand..., overcome...it".*

John 1.5

Life's fragility challenges faith,
a tiny flicker matched
against the engulfing dark.

The lottery of conception
combines the genes
in unpredictable alliance;
millions of other 'Might-have-beens'
are washed away.
Hazards attend the birth.
Disease, accident, starvation, war
continue the precariousness of existence,
yet with an unbroken line
the human race proliferates through history.
Each individual struggles into life,
gift and miracle,
embodying the promise of creation
against all odds.

Peace too is vulnerable,
its spark stamped under the jackboot;
its star, blasted from the sky
by missiles mis-called Patriot,
with warheads synthesised from
the resentments of a vicious past.
How can Serb and Croat, Jew and Arab,
Orange and Green, pair
to nurture a living reconciliation?

Perestroika conceived
a dream of peace
The infant possibility was wrapped
near to smothering in ethnic flags,
while international financers

drove nails into its over-priced crib.
Arms traders danced
the mazurka of the fairy Caraboss,
presenting christening gifts of hand grenades.

In the West
accountants' figures
displaced health or happiness
as values on the bottom line.

From fear of the impending tragedy
we close our eyes,
choosing the soft darkness
because reality is too harsh.
Age breeds foolishness,
a wisdom watching for too many threats.

Only God in the child dares
to light the Christmas hope
and carol to the uncomprehending dark.

THE RESPONSIBILITY OF GOD

(I) IN THE SHADOW OF HIS HAND

This is your world, Father.
"Bright and beautiful", the children sing;
"Full of flowers and Sun", the teacher tells them.
But is it true or just a pious hope?

For some life's day may dawn
all warm with summer.
But November comes – the cold chill
of the impending operation,
the hard winds of competition with the bills to pay,
the fog that chokes you, when love seems a cheat.

Others are born already in the grip of winter,
the unwanted child,
the baby nursed to the sound of falling bombs
while the village burns,
Limbs that have never formed,
Hungry mouths that have only sucked at Famine's breast.

O Lord why is Man brought into a place of sorrow,
born in tears or finding his way into the darkness
as the days go by?
We call you Maker, praise your power,
But yet there is more hurt than kindness
in the sum of things.
Where is the answer if your name is Love?

Be still and watch!
The sun in its eclipse
mirrors the blackness of a good man's death.
One more disaster!
But in the utter gloom
is he to whom the day and night are one.

He is the light
narrowed by extinction's threat
in airless suffocation.
The flame submits to the pressure of death.
So our griefs are borne and our sorrows carried
by one who makes the reconciliation.
In a just vengeance
all the hurt men bear is loaded on God's Son.
He who made the world accepts the weight.
We have no more to say
Darkness and light are both alike
the places where we find the radiant glory of God's face.
So peace is given not in the measure of our pain or joy
but in the presence which has filled
every experience of human kind.

(II) A ROOT OUT OF DRY GROUND

Here are my tools, Lord,
have them back!
They are no good to me after the accident
I'm finished as a craftsman.
All the skill built up through the years useless,
because a drunken driver rammed my car.

I'm not the only one,
Maker of humanity,
Who comes to accuse your wastefulness.
Behind me stand frustrated millions
who feel their gifts are left to rust;
the old whose spirit battles against imprisonment
in a body no longer able to respond;
rheumatic joints fumbling the exact thrust of the needle,
watery eyes squinting at print that blurs.

Their spirit rebels against the ruthless redundancy of the flesh.
The people trapped by circumstances into work which saps
    their joy.
The routine worker who longs to leave the bench
and let his hands create the living vision.
All people wasted, unfulfilled,
ask of you, Lord, why were they formed
to be a living accusation against your purpose
That called us into being?

Weakness and strength are words we measure with –
Bearded Barabbas looked a likely lad,
One that the girls would swoon for and the troops obey.
He went his way
and no one brings to mind a thing he did.
The one whose knees gave way under the crushing wood,
the thirsty whisperer, croaking for a drink,
holds a power to command the generations.
His helplessness has overturned all our assessments.
The wasted life of the young Prince of Glory
speaks Spring to all our withered hopes.

All that is lost, he promises, will yield
a harvest.
Then to prove his word
he throws his life away in the dark garden
By the surrender, by the insults borne
he acts the truth he taught – and waits the dawn.

(III) A LAMB TO THE SLAUGHTER

Around me, on the tombstones texts are written
"Thy Will be done"
"A Holy Rest and Peace at the last".
How false they seem,
unless the mourners were glad to get granny
underground,
What is this Will that breaks one's heart?
Why is life given only to be taken back
before it's half begun?
Young men dead in the wars,
child victims of disaster,
road casualties,
sufferers who died of cancer, polio,
and all diseases that infect our flesh,
where is the justice in your fate?
Have you no rights? Must we who love you mourn
desolate for the life which never flowered,
watering the withered hope with pointless tears?

Death is no easier when it comes with age.
Still the last enemy –
Our flesh resists its touch, the failing pulse
beats on, a lone survivor manning the outpost
where all the rest have died.

Young men and old
flinch from the icy waters
which seem to separate for ever,
sucking the lonely self away from life.

There is no comfort then in words.
A God on high who tells us to be brave
or trust his power
would seem to mock the depths of what we feel.
But if he dies
as human is dead and buried;
if he goes into hell's experience
of nothingness,

then hope is valid.
Wounded and trembling, sharing all our dread
he leads the way into the deep
where we can find a birth by drowning.
No life-line holds us safe,
the agony is real, the waters come
even into our soul
the worst we feared is here
until we find that death has turned to life.
A great High Priest has made
the only sacrifice which brings conviction
by his daring of extinction:
our clawing hands are grasped by life restored.

(IV) I HAVE SPENT MY STRENGTH FOR NOUGHT

At sixty-five the pension.
Year by year I've opened up the office,
nine till five.
There's work to do;
the 'phone rings;
letters to answer, books to be kept.
The firm is satisfied. I've served them well.

The children are married now.
Our house is neat, the mortgage paid.
Last year we fitted storm-doors to the porch.
A host of birds welcome the bread-crumbs we put out for them.

We take the Daily Telegraph,
read with concern the sad state of our world;
young people taking drugs, famine in India
and the nation's flaccid economy.

We do our best,
subscribe to the National Children's Homes,
the RSPCA, the Lifeboats, and the Blind.

This Spring my brother died –
a coronary, quite unexpectedly;
all ready for retirement, and he'd gone.

Where is the justice in a life
Which takes away the pleasure you had worked to have?

Illness and death invade us,
like the weeds that sprout in the best kept gardens.
There's the greater fear,
the massive onslaught of a nuclear war
if one dare let one's mind get round to it.

Our tidy world is only on the crust:
below there's chaos – that one keeps at bay
by trying harder.
Yet in the end we lose.
Is it our fault or are we tricked by God?

How much we long to have life orderly
To find a patterned sequence
which makes its meaning plain.
What seems to face us is a jungle growth,
governed more by chaos than by reason's rule.
Nothing seems fair if we are weighing up
in an exact balance
a reward for good deeds done.
Our cherished hopes slip from us.
Ambition proves a cheat
Our righteousness secures no cosy place
tucked by the hearth of life.
What justice was there then the Teacher hung unheeded,
when the Healer's hands were nailed?

He fed the thousands
his heart wide with compassion.
It did not stop the jeers
along the way of sorrows.
His generous giving earned him no return
only the dust of death
to blind his eyes and parch his tongue.

But if you love like that,
forgiving everything
straining the head against the uncouth beam

to cheer a dying thief,
then it is clear you do not keep accounts
of more or less desert.
Your love is free,
self-sufficient in the act it makes.
Lord teach us how to live
so that we do not fear
the staring empty looks which say we have
no meaning
Give us to know within
a ground of truth on which we stand
A rock that neither circumstances nor wagging
tongue can turn to shifting sand.

(V) ACQUAINTED WITH GRIEF

Loving was your idea, Lord.
You gave us the pattern and told us to follow it.
It seemed so good a thing,
so warm and safe,
as easy as holding a baby in your arms.
But love is painful;
Sometimes the care I've offered has been thrown back.
No doubt the fault was mine.
I'd tried to reach and comfort
but I hurt instead;
like someone touching an open sore.
I've felt the shutters fall,
eyes turn from mine
and pain has made the voice sound angry
"Go away – I have no need – you hurt".
Then I have cringed and felt unwanted,
fool that I was to think my love could heal!

And there have been occasions when I've failed
Not in the giving, but refusing love.
I could not offer any more concern;
my needs came in the way and so I stopped.
Then there was the other's pain to bear,
their hurt at what I'd done,

tears that my failure brought.
Oh, why did I begin?
Better, I've felt sometimes, a hermit life;
shut where I could not fail a wife or children,
friends or those who came.
The desert loneliness at least would quarantine
my uselessness from breeding other's hurt.

Yet you have set us all
by birth and nature
in a family, a web of intricate belonging
from which there is no escape.

Love is the pain of seeing what we do
in every contact, every word or look.
Even by absence or by holding back
we are involved.
Lord, when we see this pain, what must we do?

Mother of Jesus, standing there
as the sword pierces your heart,
can you forgive a son who hurt so deep?
he has not brought you ease,
the peace of mind or comfort in old age
most parents ask for
Does such unkindness bring to mind
the bitter birth
the times when 'God's will'
seemed to mean that you must bear the loss?
Have you a mother's accusation now
against the bitter cost of love's demands?

"There have been tears –
But tears are part of love
His truth has not been soft and womanish
He knew I loved him and he asked of me
all that my love could give.
It has not been a cheap deceit or sly manipulation
which has racked my heart.
He took me at my word and by his faith
wrought in me deeps of courage and of generosity

beyond what I could ever hope to do
His love has taken me far deeper than the smiles of happiness.

He's helped me quarry joy out of the rock
He's made me to be blest in mourning
as in laughter.
He's been my treasure and my poverty
He is my Son, my death, my endless life."

(VI) HE HATH POURED OUT HIS SOUL UNTO DEATH

What is the point?
One day follows another till a year's gone by.
The years process towards the grave.
What meaning is there
to wake me in the morning ready for the day?

A job to do, ambition beckoning on
can seem to tell me life is full of hope.
Yet hope can cheat;
The mirage city slipping from the traveller's gaze.
People may gather round and with their voices
overcome the fear of nothingness,
But people go: even the nearest fades in the
dark or falls asleep at your side.

Health and wealth;
marriage, children, friends;
all the slick prescriptions
are not proof against
the knife's edge question slipping in
"Who am I?" "Are these masks I hide behind,
a lonely unloved stranger in the world?"

Mostly we can quiet the anxious doubt:
turn up the telly;
go to the pub,
ask in a friend,
take on more work.
But through the cracks of silence, it goes on.

Religion may follow if we're made that way;
Hymns A & M replace the Beatles
to drown the insistent voice.
yet still there waits the darkness
when prayer's no longer real and people only distant figures.

"Oh, God," we cry, "why have you let me down?
There's no one there to hear my cry at all!"

Lord of the wilderness,
Lord of the lonely cross,
You did not go this way to block the path
that I must tread.
I hate it, I would turn for comfort every way,
but deep within I know there waits for me
the tears, the mourning,
and the stripping off of all pretended self-sufficiency.
My maturity must accept the role of child,
a helpless infant waiting to be born
into love's day, where sorrow turns to joy.
My reputation, intellect, and skills
like paper hats discarded when the guests go home
blow pointless down the streets before the dawn.
I wore them for disguises when the party swung.

There comes a time when my true self alone
must risk the knowing, face to face,
and find acceptance.
no distant voice will call across the vault of heaven.
Deep within he speaks to tell me I stand grounded in his life
Nothing of comfort reaches from without,
Until I burst out of the tomb into the glory of the Sons of God.

SONGS TO SING

PARTICULAR occasions, weddings, funerals, saints days and celebrations have evoked various verses. The songs people sing stay with them so there's a special responsibility in putting hymns together.

(The aurhor would be happy to answer questions about music available for these words.)

WEDDING SONG

Take my hand, I want to greet you:
Welcome smiles go out to meet you,
Growing in love means growing as people,
Loving's the way to God.

Joy in finding truth together:
Happiness in sharing laughter;
Precious times when hearts beat faster;
Loving's the life of God.

Tears are part of love's tomorrow,
Hearts that care are risking sorrow.
Why is there such hurt to go thro'
When loving's the call of God?

Jesus on the cross, you're showing
Ways of love we fear to go in.
Costing so much pain to grow in,
Yet loving's the truth of God.

What you've given, Lord, we treasure
You're the love through pain and pleasure,
You can keep us true forever,
Our love begins with God.

THE PARADOX OF LOVE

"This is my body", says Jesus the lover,
"to your hands I've entrusted my life."
The giving of God is the mystery that models
the exchange between husband and wife.

Risk is the coinage of serious wedding.
If we care, then our tears make the wine
for lifting in joy to the lips that we cherish,
to pledge "I am yours, you are mine."

Pride whirls away in the dance of belonging,
rights are no longer the goal;
by the touching in trust and surrender in laughter,
Love is the wound that makes whole.

QUEEN MARGARET OF SCOTLAND

Lord of our history's days;
as kingdoms rise and fall
your diverse servants mark the ways
that sov'reign love can call.
Their prayer's mystic light,
their hands that soothe life's pain,
their justice standing firm for right
declare your mercy's reign.

Marg'ret wore Scotland's crown
to show God's royal care;
an exiled child, her heart had known
the pain that strangers bear.
So from her castle door
no orphan turned unfed,
she touched the sick and clothed the poor,
accepted in Christ's stead.

Mother of kings and queens,
she fitted them to rule
by showing what the Gospel means,
her life of prayer their school.
By claim of monarch's right
she set her hand to build
the church most pleasing in God's sight,
laws that his Law fulfilled.

Taught by your saints of old
the discipline of power,
help us to use the gifts we hold
that others' lives may flower.
When race divides, may we
serve mutual trust's increase,
then, from all prejudice set free,
share in your reign of Peace.

LOVE OVER ALL

Dawning from darkness, hope's first light,
blended opposing black and white,
shadows that shewed the sun more bright.
Contrasts blinding us, joy rebinding us,
Love over all.

After the Flood, cleansed hearts discern
in rainbow's arch and dove's return,
patterns of care from which to learn.
Mercy deploring us, mercy restoring us
Love over all.

Trapped in a conflict hatred grows,
sorting the parties, friends from foes;
words become insults, gestures blows.
Anger splitting us, peace committing us.
God give us peace.

Holding in balance gifts of grace
wrath and forgiveness take their place,
shared aspects of the father's face.
Sin disgracing us, love embracing us
Love over all.

Christ on the cross, you turned again
the traitor's kiss, the body's pain,
building a whole which can contain
evil hurting us, grace converting us;
aspects of love.

Spirit of God look through my eyes,
so they can see with love's surprise,
compassion lives and hatred dies.
Love inviting us, love uniting us,
healing for all.

SONG OF HOPE

Canto de esperanza from Brazil

Hope gets eclipsed by life's shadows,
but God is at hand to declare;
"Capture the courage and dance with the daring
of sisters whose joy is to care;
where there's injustice and brothers are striving
be generous in taking your share."

Chorus:

> God comes like joy in the morning
> He is our friend in the strife.
> Sing to the praise
> of the Lord who can raise
> our lost hopes and restore us to life.

Hope gets eclipsed by life's shadows,
but God is at hand to declare;
"Let go your anger and learn from the witness
to peace that your sisters can bear;
work with your brothers who cherish the earth
and discover the greed you must fear."

repeat Chorus

Hope gets eclipsed by life's shadows,
but God is at hand to declare;
"Bright as the sun's rays or sharp as the starshine
be sure that my light will shine clear.
Lost on a journey or lonely in sorrow,
reach out your hand, I am here."

repeat Chorus

A YOUNG MAN'S DEATH

Brightest and best of the sons of the morning,
Dawn on our darkness and banish our night.
Star of the East the horizon adorning,
Lead us your pilgrims to healing and light.

Born to affirm us as Lord of our living,
Jesus you shared all the things that we know,
Still you are with us; new sight you are giving,
When we are blind to the way we must go.

Children we laugh as the world opens to us;
Weeping we find that there's pain and there's loss,
Spirit of Jesus in darkness renew us,
Show us the meaning, the way of your Cross.

Joys that we grasp and so anxiously cherish,
Slip through our fingers and fall to the ground,
All that we risk, all we fear that might perish,
Stays in our keeping, is lost and is found.

Brightest and best of the sons of the morning,
Rise through the mists of our tears and our strife,
Rise in our hearts, let us share in your dawning,
Make us the sons and the daughters of Life.

TRANSFIGURATION

Each human life has joys to share,
Like wine our loves brim in the cup:
But matched with them are pains to bear,
Rough broken bread we gather up.

These things which make your life and mine
Were changed by Jesus when he said
His love was flowing in the wine,
His body broken in the bread.

In his new covenant we live,
Sustained by life-transforming food,
Filled with the joy his power can give,
We celebrate a world renewed.

His love accepts the selves we bring;
Our shadowed eyes awake to sight;
The cup becomes a healing spring,
Our hands receive his glory's light.

SONG FOR THE DIOCESE

Saints of the past wove a tapestried story,
Jewelled with churches and mellow with song;
Painters and poets embellished the glory,
deepened our roots, made the fellowship strong.

The dreams and the chancels have fallen to ruin
through pride of religion and folly of kings,
God's purpose remains and the Church is made new
in the grace of his love's overshadowing wings.

Rich with the treasures of past veneration,
We can set out on a path yet untrod,
Bearing the Lord to a new generation,
Missionaries, makers and mystics for God.

HOPE

Hope was rocked in the arms of Mary.
We stretch out our hands for the sign
of the Body that's broken and risen
and the laughter that's pressed from the vine.

There are times when it hurts to be human,
love and justice absorbed by the night;
but the Child never ceases the struggle,
born in us, to rekindle the light.

SAINT NINIAN

"Go", said the Lord of Light
"spread through these days forlorn
faith to make darkness bright,
news of a hope reborn."
Where legions led, the apostles trod
to win the Roman world for God.

Fearless to own their Lord,
martyrs confessed and died.
Courage and faith's accord
spread the Church far and wide,
till by the Emperor's decree
the Gospel flourished full and free.

History turns the wheel,
ashes succeed the flame;
under the Vandal's heel
Rome bore a victim's shame.
Yet as the empires rise and fall
the Crucified reigns King of all.

In an uncertain hour
Ninian's call was clear;
he preached Christ's risen power
for northern ears to hear.
The old world faded into night;
the gospel-day dawned fresh and bright.

Still from corrupted kings,
sovereignty slips away;
our selfish scramble brings
integrity's decay.
When power's perplexed and vision dies,
blow Spirit's breath, let God arise.

THE GLAMIS HYMN

Lord, of old our fathers offered
Heart's devotion, craft's design.
Here we celebrate your purpose,
Which sustains our history's line.
Consecrating our obedience
In the gifts of Bread and Wine.

Pictures of salvation's story
Teach us trust the incarnate Word.
Each apostle bears his witness,
Facing violence, terror, sword
Steadfast in the hope before him.
Promised by the risen Lord.

Down the years this household's worship
Kept faith's candle burning bright.
Scholar's mind and soldier's courage
Tended truth, maintained the right.
Watchmen confident of morning,
Servants of the Word of Light.

Pilgrim fathers, pioneering,
Fired by wisdom from above,
Share your courage, share your vision
With your children who must move
Through these end times, fraught with danger.
To the City built on Love.

GOD AS CHILD

Wise One, you made us share your delight
in the brightness of day and the myst'ry of night,
to dance with creation in shadow and sun,
till losing and finding are joined into one.

Child of Love's morning, you give us the earth,
the hills and the valleys, the spring in the turf,
the laughter and loving that brighten the way,
the hope for to-morrow that builds on to-day.

Gentle explorer, you risked being led
to the loneliest hell and then back from the dead.
When our path descends through the dark and despair,
be with us, disclosing the glory that's there.

Artist and poet, you weave into one
our dreams and our fears, you restore what's ill-done,
through contrasts creating in healing's employ
a playground for wisdom, a cradle of joy.

NOT STRANGERS BUT PILGRIMS

Sons and daughters of creation
by God's will we came to be.
Like a poet dreaming marvels
he has spun our history,
working, till from shapeless chaos
he evoked humanity.

Dark within our first conceiving
run the rifts that still divide.
Envy splits and anger hardens,
colour, gender, wealth collide;
Sov'reign nations arm for conflict,
violence thrusting peace aside.

Yet God holds his steadfast purpose
of humanity made one.
Walls were breached and bounds transcended
by the death of his own son:
and the way for love's encounter
through the Spirit's power begun.

Down the restless generations,
called of God, his church has grown.
Martyrs' heirs and prophets' children
penetrated lands unknown,
challenged by unlikeness, finding
gifts to complement their own.

Now as pilgrims on a journey,
bonded as Christ's prayer foreshowed,
reconciled from past division
we can tread a common road.
Sisters, brothers, no more strangers
each will bear the other's load.

Rich from all that we inherit,
strong with skills new worlds devise,
Father, may we serve your kingdom
under crisis-clouded skies,
confidently re-affirming
where the morning's glory lies.

DARING DANCING TRINITY

Lord, whose power has called to being
all that fills the earth below,
myriad stars beyond our seeing,
tiniest creature that we know.
Earth and air and fire and water
woven in the grand design
witness to the final meaning
of your love in human kind.

Human lives are made for sharing;
joined in trust and truth we grow,
speech or silence opening pathways
to the hearts we seek to know.
Welcome Love, by your renewal
worn out ways turn upside down;
weak is strong, success is failure
and the wise becomes the clown.

From your Self we take our nature,
Maker, Parent, Love divine.
Bound into your life we flourish,
leaves and branches of the vine.
Through the Christ we see your pattern,
life surrendered, life restored;
Echoing through all creation
sounds the Spirit's deep accord.

Love releases us for taking
one more risk than we might dare;
glory breaks through dark and danger,
shows the Lord transfigured there.
God who planted our affections,
help your gifts to grow more free
fan us in the fires of loving,
daring, dancing Trinity.

CONNECTIONS

AT the end of the day, the questions, feelings, frustrations, need to be earthed in the steadiness of the love of God.

It is in making such connections that spirituality begins and personality matures.

CONSISTENCY?

Zachariah reflects.

Priest to the Temple,
I orchestrated the clouds of incense and the choirs
to create the ambience of awe
and lead untutored spirits
into the ritual holy fear;
not like that quiet angel
who scared me stiff
and struck me dumb.
He left the miracle that daily took my breath away,
the growing lad, the son I never thought would be.

Elizabeth was changed.
Life's pattern held
except there was more bread to bake
more clothes to tend,
but each day was lit with the glow
of the startling gift
that woke us to heaven's grace
hidden in the ordinary.

We lived in a new world.
As the baby danced in the womb,
springs of song opened,
and shepherds counting flocks of angels
found glory wrapped in straw.
In tune with the time
old Simeon told religion's requiem.

The Presence hovered
sometimes beyond the edge of sight,
emerging in the paradox of joy.
We surrendered our child to the stark desert
and watched the crowds beating a highway there.
The God of our joy and gladness,
kept covenant.

The new facts assault such faith.
The Forerunner lay discarded in prison,
his questions answered with tales of miracles for others.
And now irreparably bereaved, we cry,
"Where was the angel on the night Salome danced?"

MINISTERS MEETING

A poem for Easter

Macho meeting opens with prayer.
Deploying regulation briefcases,
the committee take station
around the boardroom battle table.
Hostility, camouflaged in ritual jokes,
breaks cover.
A magazine of platitudes
kalashnikovs
the doubters
cutting a swathe to the moral high ground.
Liberals in counter-attack break against the steel
of fundamental bayonets;
a rallying pibroch
punctures on a fine-honed text.

Agenda papers soak up the invisible blood,
and the jagged edges of shattered truth
are tidied in the final benediction.

In the tenderness of twilight
he spoke the psalm
"I still my soul and make it quiet,
like a child upon its mother's breast".

Lips, cracked in battle,
closed around the nipple
of undefended grace;
he heard as through a mother's tears
the soft lament
for children who turn 'peace'

into a war-cry
and mistake the wounds they give
for acts of love.

The crescent of repentance rose,
promise of the Pascal Moon
whose light transfigures the worst betrayal
with redeeming glory.

GOOD DAY

Was it a good day?
That depends on the shape of the ideal.
What I'd set my heart on,
slipped out of my grasp.
The meeting I planned was cancelled;
I wanted to impress someone
and he looked the other way.
"No access" blocked
the road I hoped to travel.
The weather was just the sort
that makes my head ache.
Definitely not the blueprint
for a red-letter day.

But if I turn the calendar,
with a frustrated flip
or scrumple the date
and throw it in the bin,
rubbishing the day,
I've missed the point.

It did not fill my fantasy.
It gave instead space to discover
new dimensions;
a chance to change direction
and not get hung up with resentment.
Not a perfect day – but good enough to grow in.

BRIDGE OF NIGHT

Night is the bridge between yesterday and tomorrow.
How do I cross it?
Yesterday is gone: It's foolish to labour under a pack
heavy with disappointment.
Can I shed the failure of missed opportunities
or resentment about the chance I was denied
slipping them off my shoulders?
Unbind, let go, the gentle dark comes surging in
to scour the tideline.

The good that's happened needs its cleansing too.
It's fine to remember joy,
but not to let treacly nostalgia cling
so that what has been sets the standard
and diminishes what's now.

I want to travel light into the darkness.
But what's the other side?
Does tomorrow hold so much uncertainty,
    I hope it never dawns?
Or will the wakeful night provide a shadow-play
where I rehearse the failure that might come?
Fretful with future possibilities will I put at risk
    the sleep that is?

The night is now. That's where I need to be,
glad of its stillness, surrendering what's done
and what is still to do
into the care of God.
So present peace becomes the womb
From which tomorrow is born.
Goodnight – God's night.
God's peace be with us all.

PLAYTIME

It takes a kind of courage
to find time for play.
Work is what's expected; sober thoughts,
a misership of time hoarding the precious minutes.
Fun yields no dividends,
no bonuses for jokes.
Work earns the wages;
the jobless are devalued.

Computer-haunted,
we've got it wrong.
machines are made to whir and turn
faultless, precise, achieving;
the human spirit should have space to soar
to wild absurdity.
We need permission to uncage our poet.
Eyes that rest on beauty
seem ineffectual compared to hands that hammer.
Yet the time I take off
from industrious striving
to watch, enjoy my friendships, delight in touch and taste
nourish my true self.

Thank God for the dreams
in which we mount our fiery imaginations
and ride off into the misty mountains.
Night takes to task the busy day;
but why am I ashamed to claim the right to conscious play
within the waking world?

When I can sit and let my mind catch fire
I understand how God sang for fun
calling out of nothing all creation.
Wagtails bounce and flip their feathers
salmon leap,
the world turns, the planets wheel,
tiny or vast

orchestrated into a joyful tune,
the models of all making.

Dreams, imagination and God's laughter in creation
invite me out of my industrious solemnity,
to take the task of playing seriously
until my marred manhood
is recreated in the child I have denied.

THE STARTLEMENT
OF SHRINES

TRADITION offers an expected interpretation of a
holy place but history and devotion do not stand
still. I have been led to new interpretations of place
and saint that speak to my condition.

LETTER TO ST. FRANCIS

Beloved Francis

Christmas was a time that was specially dear to you. The poverty of the stable at Bethlehem fitted so well with the way that you and the first brothers lived in your small hermitages. You found yourselves most at home in the little, ramshackle places that nobody else really wanted. No wonder it was your inspiration to build a life-sized Christmas crib at Greccio. We have been setting up models ever since in our churches, our homes, in shop windows and in the market place with an infinite variety of good and bad taste. But that would not worry you. You were always the maverick, the unpredictable character, setting no store by your own reputation, turning authority upside down like the clowns in the circus.

This year has been your great eight hundredth anniversary. Assisi and all the surrounding Umbrian hills have echoed your praises. The Catholic hierarchy gathered; painting, poetry and music have celebrated your fame. Little poor man of Assisi, what do you think of the world which sets you amongst its great ones?

In the soaring basilica dedicated to you, they showed to the pilgrims the patched rags that you wore. Do you remember how cross your brothers got because you kept on giving away even the clothes you had to beggars who were worse off than you? Since then the Church has celebrated your life's story in richest art. They took the poor worn out body and buried it within not one great church, but two, one on top of the other in amazing grandeur. But when I went to sit in front of your tomb, thinking I'd find there something of the simplicity of Bethlehem, the only thing I saw was the iron lattice work that protects it. They're keeping you safe, hedging you round with the same imprisoning security within which our wealthy Western world is dying.

One night I stayed in a Convent, lost in a host of genial Dutch folk, good Catholics come to savour the holiness of the shrine. They had dined well, the wine had been red and the barley had added its blessing to the fruit of the grape.

"What about Peace?" I asked them, for peace is a good Franciscan word and it belongs also to the Christmas story which welcomes the Prince of Peace. "In your country the Churches have found a voice together in the group that is called the IKV. In Britain we have admired the strength of their witness".

"Communists" they declared "or politically naïve. These ecumenists are not to be trusted".

Do they pray for peace, I wondered, yet hope that it never comes because it might be too demanding to love one's neighbour?

The authorities have produced a book for your birthday "Francis, Man of Peace". Is it safe to call you that because your body is behind the iron bars?

Beloved Francis, I've thought of you in the olive groves beside San Damiano, where you first heard the Voice. I've breathed the woodland air high in the hills at La Verna where you found the space to pray. Am I being sentimental when I find your spirit there rather than in the great buildings and institutions? You found your inspiration in the picture of the humble stable: you followed the Son of Man who never had an established home. Did you preach to the birds because even in your day what you had to say was too difficult for people to hear?

How am I really to honour your memory today, my beloved brother? We have so little time left for our world to hear the word of Peace. We've boxed ourselves in the iron grilles of weapons, suspicion and wealth. We can only hear distorted voices beyond the ghetto we've made in the name of liberty. We fear the poor nations because they challenge our comfort: we fear the powerful because they threaten our security. We have brought the world to the brink of destruction through our science and our pride. Child of a deaf generation, I need to hear your preaching to me through the birds. They can fly over the wire, across national boundaries; they can bring messages when the air waves are jammed, their soft wings scoop under the satellite's surveillance. Help me to see with fresh eyes the sparrows, the swallows, the hawks and the doves that are part of the poetry of creation so that they can call me back to the forgotten visions of the world where children play in trustfulness, where suspicion is not the mark of the wise and successful but of the hurt and the sick who must be loved back to fellowship. Help me to kneel in the straw and discover the security which comes from giving things away and having open doors.

In the end it is the imagination of men and women which must be kindled by such signs and symbols so that they are aflame with a new obedience to be instruments of Peace. So I must travel the world like the migrant swallows, claiming every country, every political system for God. I must live in the security of the sparrows whom Jesus chose as the symbol of a whole creation that is sustained by a Father's loving will. Above all, I must enjoy the world so much that I can be an inspired opportunist building a nest in the security of his presence, not fretfully labouring at shelters and silos, like the dead Pharaohs' pyramids, to protect myself or to destroy others.

Beloved brother, your work began with the call to rebuild a Church which had become weak in its witness, shabby in the reflection of God's glory. Once again, Christ's people are tongued-tied. We live amid a generation that is demented with its grandiose claims to usurp the control of this planet's future and with the fears that arise from the possession of such power. In your centenary year, laugh us into humility, love us into compassion so that we can share with the poor, make peace among the powerful and teach human kind to sing again the praises of God who created us all to be one and brings us to our senses by being born in poverty and helplessness.

Assisi, 1982

OUTPOST OF HISTORY

High as the eagles, the castle
dominates the valley;
below, checkpoint on the ascending road,
the old guardpost emerges through the soil.
Stones, dressed by Roman skill to oppose the enemy,
support a botanist's delight.

Yellows shade through marigolds to buttercup to fennel.
Iris, bugloss, alkanet, glow purple.
Clovers, vetches and species beyond my repertoire
share their brilliance with the poppies.

It is a place to fidget the painter's brush
to creativity.
The colours weave a spell for meditation;
But beyond the eye's response
the seeds, nectar, pollen, petal,
build a hidden chain to nourish
another system where insect or bird
thrives ruthlessly on another's death.

Just as the bee-eaters swoop and crunch their prey,
the centuries have swallowed in their turn
Roman watchmen, Visigoth supplanters,
Moorish victors and Christian lords
to build the subsoil of my reality.
In the genetic lake of human stock
I am kin to all,
our doings receive and transmit a common heritage.

Unnoticed as the lizard, in his minute contribution
to the eco-system,
I too can add an anonymous pebble
to the cairn of conscious care
securing the unborn future.

                                        Gaucin, Spain

SPANISH CHURCH

The notice penned by priestly piety
invited visitors to reverence;
the small flame signalled the Presence
el Santissimo;
"Kneel here, adore!"

The familiar phrases resonated.
The god of the Holy Bread
has sired generations of sermon cliches
as clergy magnified their office.

Suddenly the stones
demanded redress.
Their holiness was bred
by the pulsating echoes
of those whose vision had danced
for beauty;
of worshippers who came
to celebrate the pain of birth or sing of death;
of lovers discovering the mystery
of bodies' touch;
of minds that wrought in doubt
a subtle scaffold for faith.

The sanctity of history
blazed through the building
to quench the self-important candles
and proclaim the human glory
to an inverted theology of things.

Yet the priest who left the legend
beneath the evocative Mozarabic arches
also has his place,
his particular devotion
enriching the embroidery of times remembered.
Only his demanding certainties
must accept the discipline of variegation

Religion has no answers.
Its light flickers
to entice complacency
to pilgrimage
and ensure

we do not escape the hard questions
which alone breed meaning
from the perplexing union
of birth and death.

Santa Maria de Lebeña, Los Picos, Spain

IONA: WOMB FOR A NEW AGE?

Abbey or fortress?
Garrisoned by the encircling sheep
are your cloisters fenced
to shelter a fragile faithful?
Or is your table set
with banqueting rites for all
who stir at the quest
of being?

When gnostic intellect,
born again to a New Age, knocks
should outraged divinity bar the door?
Beyond the wall
will demons snare
the incautiously inquisitive?
Or has faith designed an open house
to fold the thoughtfully deviant
and the unbridled pilgrim?

There is a confidence in questions,
Ancient wisdom lights torches
to probe the shadows of hidden places
not mark salvation's flare path.
Fear cries "crusade!"
and under the banner of assurance
rallies the anxious to the ramparts
against the insurgent Spirit.

Heritors of the open sky,
the fellowship of the Dove
lift, wheel and play,
wings spread to catch the wind
that blows
over the risky deeps of liberty.

Iona, 1990

THE MYSTERY OF FAITH

Dissonance of the generations unsettles faith.
Taught by the original Gospels, child of to-day,
I struggle to plumb ancestral devotion,
expressed in the brocaded sovereignty of the Holy Child.
In the sacristy, Santo Nino's wardrobe
intricately embroidered,
gold on blue, white or crimson,
evokes admiration confused with laughter.

Once an emperor's greed sent soldiers
to demand the church's treasures.
Laurence the Deacon displayed the true riches,
the poor and old, faithfully at prayer.
The confused authorities capped the paradox
by adding Laurence to the treasury of martyrs.

Converted kings reversed the tariff
and gilded their shrines
with the spoils of the oppressed.

Last of the line, I bring my questioning pen,
at least as much to win
approval from the critically insightful
as to find my way into adoration.

As best we can, we bring our offerings,
to build our half-relatedness into faith's surrender.
Museums of piety,
the churches house the intermediate aids,
mistaken for divinity.

Only God knows which souls deceived themselves
and which played with such abandon
that they found their toys transfigured
and their hearts grown pure enough to see.

                    The Church of Santo Nino, Gaucin, Spain

JAMES THE GREATLY MISREPRESENTED

Mother never understood
When John and I dissolved the family partnership
to follow the disciple's path
we felt the protective framework
of the old way, crack.
She hoped we'd better ourselves.
Just put in a word, she said,
to book a place at court under King Jesus.

Herod make the same mistake,
treating me to execution
like an important leader.
Not quite the honour mother imagined;
they say I smiled to receive death's accolade.

Simplicity makes uninteresting telling.
The legend-makers' package
had toured Thomas in India
taken Peter to Rome
given John adventures;
the chroniclers needed a better story
for Zebedee's other son.
Or perhaps a mother's spirit inspired
the Spanish matrons
to make her Jamie 'Great'.

Myth matched the military needs.
Visigoths and Moors
had wasted the first flowering of Iberian sanctity,
then in a star-drenched field
they opportunely found my bones!
Eight centuries had healed
Herod's sword cut
and veiled the fisherman's past.
Mother's dream knight,
I rode out on a royal charger
to hack the infidel.

Miracle-struck,
the pilgrims of Europe,
with staff and cockle-shell,
took the highway of faith to Santiago.

In the Renaissance dawn
brilliant with new worlds, new knowledge,
the glory dimmed.
Finally the English cannon, broadsiding heresy from
    seaward
panicked the bishop.
Forgetting my victories,
he was content to salvage the relics.
Smuggled into safe-keeping, the bones were lost.
Iago might have been translated back to Galilean James
and mother's dream have faded.

The hierarchy refused demobilisation,
Secret weapons forged by Science
were assaulting the soul of Europe.
In a fresh Crusade,
the Revelation which once rolled Moorish heads
must silence tongues too quick to question.
Mother Church would sit enthroned,
trimming the over-clever Faculties,
clipping political wings.

To meet the need, the bones were found again,
authenticated by papal scholarship,
acclaimed across the oceans.
In a new tone Compostella summons the pilgrims;
Solemn days are set
with Holy Years to multiply the tally of forgiveness.
The Way is structured with stations, stamping
    certificates of piety.
But as the pilgrims travel I whisper hints of God,
met in the fun of exaggerated stories
and the generous mutual care of blistered feet.
"Watch for the birds; celebrate the streams,
remember the fellowship of the Fish".

At the Feast rumbustious fireworks
do duty for miraculous stars.
The Mass is filled with music and they swing
the absurdness of the Censer
to rock religion into laughter.

Then I recall five thousand picnickers,
the same gusts of conviviality
subverting matriarchal management.
The Master allowed no partiality.
His justice commanded us to feed
the undeserving poor.
Perhaps a peasant fisherman knows best
to lead a universal pilgrimage,
giving victors and victims evenhandedly
a shell's glory for sufficient decoration;
reminding ambitious mothers
that the last are first.

Santiago de Compostella, 1990

END PIECE

THE last word is mostly with the Angels.

CELEBRATE THE THIRD AGE

Those who are planted in the House of the Lord,
shall flourish in the courts of our God.
They shall still bear fruit in old age,
they shall be green and succulent.

Psalm 92 vv. 12,13

I've seen withered roots, clawing on to life
in soured soil;
spindly branches, brittle with frustration,
ready to crackle when anger strikes.
This is the desert of the unfertile intelligence,
swept by the bitter music of the piper
for whom nobody danced.
Half liberator, jackal Death
waits to crunch the carcass, dried to an untimely end
by disappointment.

Jewels of fruit glisten on other trees
that tap into deep reservoirs of being.
Watered by affection, they blossom
in the spring time of maturity.
At home in the delight of God
they express the green glory of creation;
to the last, the sap rises
and laughter stirs in the supple leaves.

HARK THE GLAD SOUND

"Thank you everybody," said the Archangelic conductor of the
choir, "same time tomorrow."

It was the last rehearsal before the annual performance. A
young tenor seraph was looking perplexed and risked an
interruption.

"Just before we go, I'd like to suggest that the line 'On earth,
his peace' gets increasingly urgent, yet even the believers don't

take it very seriously. Isn't there some way to draw attention to the message? When we actually appeared to the shepherds it shocked them into action, could that be repeated?"

There was a chorus of "Hear, hear" from the cherubs in the harp section.

"I'll enquire", promised the Archangel.

The proposal was approved in a modified form and by the miracle of Heavenly Telecom it was arranged for the performance to be beamed direct to the subconscious of anyone whose attention was tuned to the wavelength of prayer or deep longing.

Ronald lay awake, pondering the likely New Year comments about a "lame duck President" as he began to run downhill to the end of his term of office. Perhaps "lame duck" stuck in his mind because the turkey was giving him indigestion. "I wish…" he began and as though he had pressed the button there was singing and the heavenly vision crowded in on him.

"I knew it!" he cried, "My dream was true. We can get peace by putting a shield up there. That angel routine has always been telling us simple guys something we need to know – Peace is in orbit. Get Jerry Falwell, get Schultz, get Weinberger and God bless America!"

Gorbachev was looking at the night sky and longing to be free from the political struggle. So many battles to be won at home and abroad. His Russian soul was lifted by the music. "That's it! We have underestimated the arts. In every Socialist country there is a Peace Committee but their message is visibly propagandist. Satellites give us the chance to beam something different around the world, to create a new image of socialist man, We must recruit more music, poetry, perhaps even religion to paint an icon of Russian Peace that will capture the imagination of the workers."

In Beirut and Belfast two similar activist cells had just paused to contemplate the effect of the campaigns they had outlined. For Shi'ite and I.R.A. men alike the flaming sky was a sign. "Mao said, 'Power comes from the barrel of a gun' – I tell you, brothers and sisters, that Peace is born out of the blast of a bomb."

The Prime Minister could not believe her ears. Here were

voices picking up the very theme she had so clearly articulated on that first triumphant day at Downing Street when she had quoted St. Francis' prayer. She had stuck to it through Falklands campaign and economic crisis. Reconciliation was there for all who had the good sense to see things her way. Heartened by the assurance that the magnificent choir had grown from the small enterprise of the original group of seven Archangels, she waved them on their way and, calling "Rejoice" made a mental note to consider the possibility of a new market for British instrument manufacturers.

"I could have told you what would happen," said the bishop, addressing the light that now hovered round his cathedral. "Human beings are not pure intelligence, as mediaeval philosophers thought angels to be. We distort any message that we receive, consequently you get represented as feathered futilities and the god of religion can become a dangerous reinforcement of our prejudices."

A journalist who overheard hurried off to file an exclusive story "Bishop warns angels not to believe in God".

"Of dear!" sighed a cherub hanging up his harp, "not a great success. Next year we'd better settle for the old style communication, and leave it to a few frail human beings to be the peace messengers."

"After all, " said the Archangel, "that was the Original Plan".

Christmas 1988

OVERHEARD IN HEAVEN

"I sometimes wonder if they'll make it" said the Archangel as he folded his wings for what passes in celestial circles as a coffee break.

It was the department of Future Options and the section concerned with planet earth had become decidedly worried.

"Do you think they'll start a nuclear war?" asked a trainee cherub.

"Probably not" replied the senior Archangel, "though we have built that possibility into our contingency plans. But that is a danger that they recognised. The real threats are the ones they don't notice. They are so ingenious and yet so blind that they seem to be working for their own destruction".

The staff of the office had often observed the new technological discoveries and then been appalled at the use to which they had been put. Recently they had discussed the brilliant medical advances.

"They seem to manage life and death as effectively as the Omnipotence", said one of the under-angels.

"They lack his ability to say "No", said another, "Saving life flatters their sense of power. They have no judgement to see when their excited 'Yes' is no longer expedient. They have that destructive kind of pride which makes them believe they can cope with whatever crises they manufacture".

"Isn't that why they're so attractive? They have a kind of terrible innocence which lets them go where we are afraid to travel."

"Courage is one thing, irresponsibility is another" – it was the senior Archangel speaking again – "Their knowledge has taken them to the place where they have got to learn to be responsible for one another or perish. That's why I sounded so pessimistic just now".

"But look at what they have accomplished. They have peopled the earth and then filled it with all the creations of their minds. Look at how they have got in touch with one another, sharing ideas across continents and reaching out beyond the earth. If they want it they have the possibilities of every kind of enterprise. Besides that, they can learn to understand each other and bring up their children to live as one family all around the globe.'

"That's one of the options on the files" replied the senior. "It's the dream we put into their heads when they pause to ask for direction. It's the way we nudge events whenever we can. The trouble is that the future is theirs to make. Have you looked at the alternative stories? They make your wing-feathers tingle".

"I have" said another angel whose halo went pink with compassion. "If I were one of them, I'd weep for the sheer frustration of seeing the possibility taken away. They've discovered that they belong to one another, yet use their skills for manipulating and exploiting the weaker. They have all the means of sharing their dreams and their hopes. Instead they live by competition. They have got the technology to fulfil the highest predictions and they use it for greedy production. They do not ask as we do, where they are going. They simply want more for tomorrow.

"They get power over each other by promising the impossible. That little planet will not be able to bear the weight of their ambition as every nation demands more resources for energy and exhausts the life forces. They are damaging the delicately balanced system so that it will no longer be able to renew itself".

"Have you ever seen one of them subject to that disease they call cancer?" asked the Archangel. "It's when a group of cells begins to multiply malignantly within the total system of the human body. They take over without regard for the other parts which nourish them and so they become a fatal disease. Looking at that delicate economy that once was sung into being by love it looks as though that's what's happening to the earth. It's another option we keep on the files'.

"But surely the Omnipotence is not going to stand helplessly by? Once before he uttered a Word which changed the course of things".

"The channels are still open" responded the senior "But it seems so hard to get through. Let me show you a tiny example."

He reached forward and manoeuvred into position what was obviously a piece of celestial technology designed to focus the wide-ranging vision of an angel. Gothic pillars swam into view. It was Canterbury Cathedral.

"Makers of heaven and earth and of all things seen and unseen" the voices of five hundred bishops gathered for the Lambeth Conference affirmed their faith.

"Watch" said the archangel as near to exasperation as it is possible for his kind to be. "There are people who've been given the chance to know what it's about and even they miss the point. They gathered world-wide to talk together. They had a sense of crisis. These were voices declaring 'The end is nigh!' but would you believe it, they were addressing the wrong apocalypse. They thought that having women bishops was the end of the world!"

"Their foolish self-centred theology blocked their ears to the real crisis of humanity. they were so obsessed by their sexual fantasies that they could not find time to pay attention to the ravages of the disease which is invading human sexuality. One archbishop spoke clearly and directly. He had counted the cost of the medical facts but nobody else really noticed.

When that passed them by it was not surprising that they were deaf to the rape of the natural world. It can only speak through signs which are easily ignored; the bird song which falls silent, the sun growing unaccustomedly hot, the oceans carrying poison instead of food."

"Does it need to be like that?" asked the cherub.

"Of course not; the end is not yet written. There's all the power of love to will that it should not be so, but a choice has to be made. The politicians have no time to tackle the large unpopular issues. They are too busy making sure that they get re-elected. The bishops have a chance to think widely and speak clearly. They are a kind of people who could help the choice. Within the plan, the Omnipotence has provided his own trans-national bodies, if only they can lift their noses beyond local anxieties to offer faith to the world."

"I saw things being written down on paper" said the hopeful angel. "Won't the bishops remember those when they get home and are not distracted by reporters asking the wrong questions?"

Lambeth Conference, 1988

PROMISES, PROMISES

"A promised land?" asked Abraham,
"Travel and a cloud of descendants;
are you sure?"
"It's guaranteed" said the angel,
keeping the time scale secret.

Fighting and famine
eventually led the way to Egypt,
fulfilment still deferred.
Miracles and plagues launched the return,
but being 'chosen' palled.
"We would have done better to miss the trip.
Brick-makers' rations were frugal,

but better than alternating starvation
with quail and manna sandwiches."
Does God write hidden codicils to Covenants?

"It's definite" the prophet Nathan assured King David,
"a throne with a future".
Yet Absalom's rebellion sent the old king
flying as a refugee.
Next, Solomon, for all his wisdom
reduced the heritage,
bequeathing his heirs
the smaller half of a split kingdom.

Five hundred years,
the promises, elusive as will-o'-the-wisp,
danced ahead.
Exile followed conquest
while anxious prophets defended God's consistency,
excusing the delay
by the weight of Israel's sins;
reserving generosity
exclusively for the deserving.

Prayer and repentance earned no enlightenment
as the generations rolled.

Then came the disconcerting Birth.
Though later gospellers embroidered the story
with hints of royalty,
the neighbours never guessed that Joseph's lad
hid the son of David.
Village gossips, savouring the scent of scandal,
had no suspicion of the Covenant's heir,
incognito in Nazareth.
Explanation is hindsight's business.

Ambiguous angels
set Mary trembling;
struck Zachariah dumb;
scared the shepherds
with supernatural light and music:
prophesies of further "good news"
to swallow!

Messiah sharpened the paradox,
blessing poverty and persecution,
assuring the marginalised, the meek,
the mourning, the merciful,
how lucky they were.
Healer and teacher
awarded a mock coronation,
whipped and worshipped,
above his victim's throne,
fluttered the satiric title
of the occupying power.

We deck the story with fairy lights and carols,
marketing the unique Divine Offer.
Yet still our deprived communities
shudder with violence;
empty hands stretch out from Africa;
the abandoned Bosnians plead
for food before the worst of winter.
The drone of moralists,
championing family values
drowns out cries from the neglected cot.

For children, a promise is kept
when the surprise emerges from its wrappings
on Christmas morning.
Do we expect to untie
bows around prescriptive intervention
limiting our choice?
Can we appreciate the unconfining gift
of space to build salvation
in the cancer ward,
or among the ruins of Beirut?
Obsessed by the rich pigments of Old Masters,
lacking the accustomed cobalt tinted robes,
we fail to glimpse the Virgin
shielding the glazed eyes of her son
from the intrusive flies of Africa.
The ash of naked tragedy
carries no hint of embers to be rekindled.

Perplexing promise, you offer no solution,
but a presence that weaves glory
into the rough resentment, the cries and anguish,
of each day's events.
The dream-given name 'Emmanuel' beats its coded
    message;
an infant smile embracing the unlike;
a song inviting enemies to dance;
with us till the end of time,
unveiling the secret of the God within.

We, and not some other 'they',
must spin the wheel of birth and resurrection,
mend the riven tree,
make the world one home to share:
ourselves the Gift of God,
the future hope that makes the journey's end,
the promised dawn.

SECOND ROUND?

Christmas is over
its tinselled gifts exposed,
our thanks genuinely expressed
or awkwardly withheld
for whisky, woolly hat, unwanted novel.

There remains the Child
symbol of gratuity, grace-given, undemanding,
yet capable of calling out
self's total surrender, immolation love-wrapped.

Can his appeal
transform history-obsessed brutality
bitter, ready to rend
the new-born hopes of fragile peace
to score a political point?

Weapons, consecrated to an idol Cause
may blast the way to partisan advantage
but reprisals follow.
Death upon death disfigures
Belfast, Jerusalem, Cape Town and every place
where High Priests of Justice
offer the Holocaust of violence
to a blood-hungry state.

Perhaps the God who puts himself at risk
requires another Birth and Death;
angelic scouts seek volunteers
to cast a Second Coming
for a New Year of good hope.